LOOKING BACK AT
ALTRINCHAM

Basil D Morrison

Willow
PUBLISHING

People will not look forward to Posterity
who never look backward to their ancestors.

Edmund Burke.

While often asked to do so over the years, I would never presume to produce a lengthy and detailed history of the Town of Altrincham. This has already been done most successfully by numerous noteworthy historians previously.

In this jet age of the 80's in which we live, I felt that an easily assimilated speedy referencer might be more useful to the newcomer to the area and the older resident alike.

It should, despite certain omissions and perhaps the odd unintended inaccuracy, act as a brief and illustrated historical guide only to be used as a point of departure for a much more detailed study in depth.

If this publication should prove helpful in any way, then my enthusiasm for such an absorbing subject has made its presentation not only justifiable but a heartfelt pleasure.

This is not however to belie the truth of the statement made by a little cripple girl on Altrincham to Mrs. Gaskell in her book "The Three Ears" . . . "Mother, if Heaven is not as beautiful as this place, I don't want to go there".

Basil D Morrison Bowdon 1980

ISBN 0 9506043 5 6

Willow Publishing, Willow Cottage, 36 Moss Lane, Timperley, Altrincham, Cheshire, WA15 6SZ
Printed by The Commercial Centre Ltd., Clowes Street, Hollinwood, Oldham

The Map is reproduced from the original in the Local History Collection, Altrincham Library by kind permission of the Borough of Trafford Library Service.

The Author offers his real thanks to all those who have contributed towards the making of this book and for advice, loan and use of photographs.

If through obscurity of ownership or in-advertence, any rights still surviving have not been acknowledged the author humbly hopes that the owners will pardon the omission.

George Street about 1900.

CONTENTS

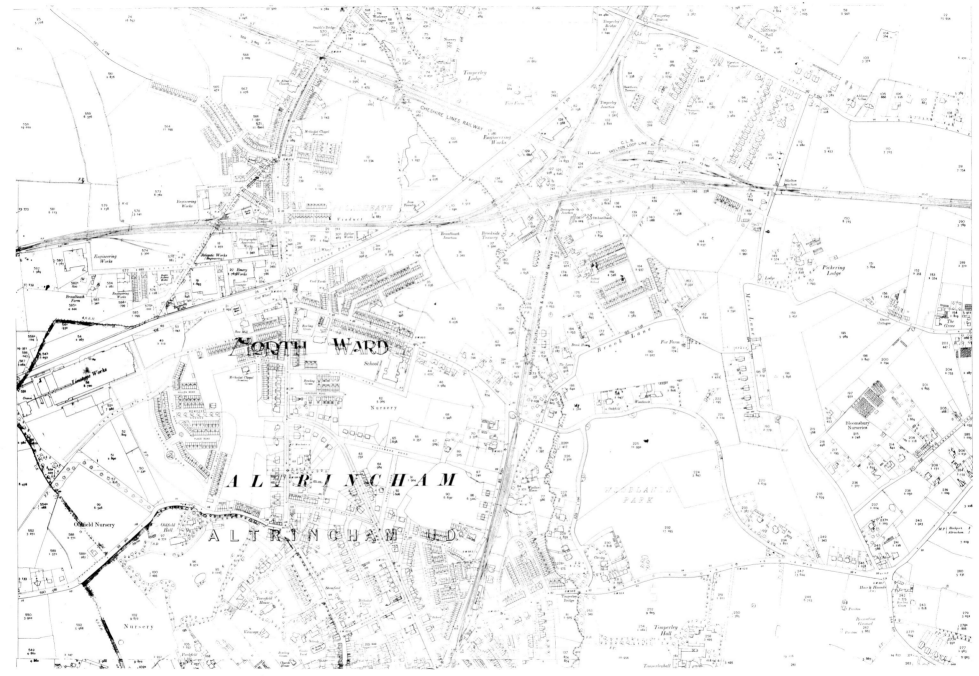

1910 map of Altrincham and district. See also end cover.

Altrincham – some thoughts on its name.

The story of Altrincham, with its very proud history tailing back to Saxon times, must surely be a mixture of fiction, truth, history, tradition and opinion if the historians are to be our guide in this. Indeed he would be a courageous person who would dogmatise as to how Altrincham came to be so named.

Firstly, as to the spelling. In the towns Charter of 1290, reference is frequently made to Altringham, spelled with a 'G' and from Gravestones in the area it seems this form of spelling continued into the 16th and 17th centuries, when the letter 'C' appeared to become common useage, possibly due to the illiteracy of Parish Clerks at the time.

Dorothy Sylvester in her 'History of Cheshire' is of the view that the earliest points at which Anglo Saxons settled in any district can be traced by the spelling "---ING" as in Hastings. This suggests the original settling places of the clan, whereas when a prefix and suffix, as in ALT and HAM are respectively added, such places could be off-shoots from the main clan or tribe. ALT is a Roman word,

suggesting a hilly place, so that this prefix was appropriate to Altrincham, enjoying elevated views Northwards across the Moss and Mersey valley beyond. "HAM" indicates an enclosure or a family home, again appropriate to this area.

On the other hand Dodgson believes this may be the village of ALDHERE'S People; HAM is a homestead or village. The medial may be INGA Gen(itive) of INGAS "The People of".

However, Altrincham and Kermincham, Tushingham, Warmingham and Wincham, all belong to a class of place names exhibiting the Birmingham – BRUMMADGEM – phenomenon, a palatalized and assibilated medial – ING, supposed to be variants of –INGA compounds with the alternative INGIA form.

Altrincham would then be Alderinge-ham, in which Alderinge means 'at the place (called) Aldhering i.e., named after Aldhere.

While I personally favour Dodgsons views and only a few incline towards Chas. Nicksons somewhat legendary but nevertheless rather romantic opinion as to Tring and his journey Northwards, we cannot for certain say that some basic truth may not be buried beneath some invented falsehood.

Altrincham Station

It is interesting to note that on the Township Map of 1852 two stations are shown as existing at the time. The earliest and first station was called Altrincham Station and was sited close to the present level crossing, but on Friday 21st June 1849 Altrincham and Bowdon Station was opened on land fronting upon Railway Street, but set well back from the street. However, in 1880 with the advancement in industry, it was decided to open up what is now Stamford New Road and erect a new station in its present position, including the Station Clock, still preserved.

The Venus was the first engine on the Railway and 65 passengers made that momentous journey. The fares at that time were:–

First Class (single) Express	*One shilling (5p)*
First Class (single) Ordinary	*10d*
Second Class	*8d*
Third Class	*6d*

When the tramway ceased to exist in 1931, the Railway was electrified from London Road, Manchester, to Altrincham.

A row of single storey shops was erected about 1895 along that side of Railway Street as we know it today. The old station at the rear remained there until about 1965–1970 as a carriage shed, when it was demolished. The whole of this land extending eastwards to a point where it joined Hale Moss was known as The Pinfold. Lloyd Street, named after Jeremiah Lloyd, who built Lloyds Fever Hospital in 1850 for £600 on land given by Lord Stamford, was originally known as Pinfold Brow.

The shop premises at the corner of Lloyd Street (Lanterns) was a Temperance Hotel in the 1850's.

Two trams after a collision on Washway Road, near the Hovis Recreation Ground.

Trams in Altrincham

Another valuable link between Altrincham and Manchester was forged on 9th May 1907, when the first tram made its slow way through crowds of sightseers from the foot of the Downs. Trams became very popular and were used by many thousands of people.

The lines were leased by the District Council to Manchester Corporation Tramways for 23 years, on the expiration of which, due to the coming of the omnibus services, the last tram departed from Altrincham on 6th June 1931.

Behind the row of single storey shops, built about 1895 and very little changed today, lay the original Altrincham and Bowdon Railway Station unused by passengers after 1880 but which was used as a carriage repair shed and depot, clearly seen from Goose Green Bridge, until some years ago when it was demolished.

It is noteworthy that for 1d you could travel by tram from the Downs to Park Road, Timperley and also the later trams to Deansgate were numbered 48, which was continued by the bus services up to recent times.

A 48 tram at the Terminus in Railway Street, Altrincham.

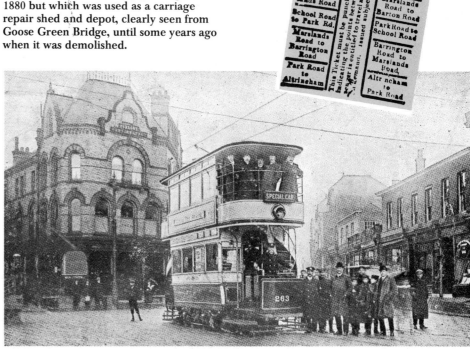

The First Tram to Altrincham 30 April 1907.

Stamford New Road and Station Buildings

Railway Street was extended into Stamford New Road about 1880 to give access to the new station, and to do this a number of old buildings had to be demolished including Thomas Faulkner's thatched cottage, more than 200 years old (in whose memory the Faulkner's Arms Inn was erected on the opposite side of the road near Stella Brooks shoe shop).

The adjoining Orange Tree Inn was also demolished at the same time, the name being transferred to the premises opposite The Unicorn Hotel, Old Market Place – The Orange Tree Inn.

On part of what was once the site of the original Orange Tree Inn, was built The Stamford Hotel which was burned down, rebuilt again in Victorian style and finally demolished about 1965 to make way for the Graftons Development.

In 1905 J. H. Broun built Station Buildings, an imposing office block. He also built Altrincham G.P.O. and adjoining shops known as Moss Burn buildings to the design of a well known local Architect, John McNamara. Station Buildings contained at least 84 offices and the building was the first of its type, hitherto unknown in Altrincham. Notice too that at this time Bonson's still owned the shop at the corner of Moss Lane, later sold to the Midland Bank.

H. GRANGE,

CHEMIST, DRUGGIST,

AND FAMILY TEA DEALER, GROCER, &c.

NO. I. CHURCH-ST. & MARKET-PLACE,

Adjoining the TOWN HALL,

ALTRINCHAM.

Begs to tender her acknowledgments to her Friends and a discerning public for the unlimited confidence which has been so long reposed in her, and respectfully solicits a continued share of their favours, assuring them no exertion shall be spared on her part calculated to merit their Patronage and Recommendation. She warrants every Article sent from her Establishment to be of the most SELECT and GENUINE quality—That all Preparations and Compounds are made in strict accordance with the different Formula directed by the College of PHYSICIANS &c. Every Prescription, Family Receipt, &c. shall be compounded with the most Scrupulous Accuracy, Punctuality and Dispatch.

A LARGE ASSORTMENT OF PATENT MEDICINES, PERFUMERY,

HAIR, TOOTH, AND NAIL BRUSHES.

WINDSOR, HONEY & OTHER FANCY SOAPS.

AGENT FOR

SCHWEPPE'S AND OTHER SODA AND ALKALINE WATERS.

CARRARA WATER, CHAMPAGNE, LEMONADE, &c.

FARINA'S EAU DE COLOGNE.

EVERY KIND OF

GARDEN, FLOWER AND AGRICULTURAL SEEDS.

Advertisement for H Grange, No 1 Church Street. (See page 11)

In 1965, at the corner of George Street and what was then High Street, stood this row of very old cottages (now the site of Tesco Supermarket). Comprised in this Row was The Old Cafe, a Tripe Shop, a Boot Repairers and a Jewellers Shop, and others, all owned originally by Miss Berry who lived at "Parklands" Charcoal Road, Bowdon. Her father, William Berry, was a Boot Blacking manufacturer in Manchester and to this day his product "Cherry Blossom" boot and shoe polish, named after his daughter, is still obtainable in the shops.

The Old Market Place

The site of the original Saxon settlement, it acted as a hub from which the town radiated in later years. Sir Walter Scott in his book "Peveril of the Peak" gives a colourful description of Julian Peveril on his journey from Liverpool to Derbyshire when he halted at the Cat and Fiddle, better known as the Red Lion Hotel (see left of picture). It was to this Inn that Prince Charles. the Pretender's troops came in December, 1745, demanding billets on their way to Macclesfield.

The adjoining Inn, The Horse and Jockey, derived it's name from an earlier building

bearing the same name, owned at the time by Robert Boardman, who combined his activities as Publican with that of Horse Breeding. The Bay Malton, an Inn at Seamons Moss Bridge was named after a horse of that name bred by him and belonging to the then Lord Stamford.

The shop beyond, for many years occupied by Trevors the french polishers, has now been skilfully incorporated with the Orange Tree Hotel at the end of the row. Although shown on a township map of 1852 as a building on the site, it did not become a Pub until about 1880, when the original Orange Tree Inn (later the Stamford Hotel in Stamford New Road) was burned down and the licence and name transferred to

Old Market Place. It stands close to a passage leading to Leslie Arnold's Old Cattle Mart, previously Goodalls, the removers and storers.

The whole of this side of the Market Place was occupied by houses of similar size, including a Pub called the Waggon and Horses, which was demolished to make way for the building of Lloyds Bank in 1877 and the opening of Dunham Road as we know it today. Market Street was then known as High Street, which extended to Stamford Estate Office, where it turned right and became known as Dunham Road, thence joining the Turnpike Road, we now know as Dunham Road.

The larger portion of what we now know as The Unicorn Hotel, was erected by Lord Stamford in 1849 and was the original Town Hall with Council Chamber, and a prominent clock and Bell Tower, a facsimile of which adorned the roof of the old Butter Market. The Town Bell was given originally in 1684 by Lord Delamer and now hangs on the staircase of the Unicorn Hotel. The new Town Hall in Market Street was erected about 1900.

Old Market Place is a conservation area containing listed buildings now protected against demolition without consent.

The Title Page picture shows a closer and later view of Bowden and Parkes shop and house near the corner of Old Market Place and Post Office Street, in the garden of which was built David Morrison's offices by William Cunliffe Brooks, below which on Kingsway, Mr. W. H. Parkes built a fine block of shop property, part of which was until about 1978/79 used as a temporary library, pending the opening of the existing library in Stamford New Road. This area was often referred to in those days as Higher Town or Quality Corner.

Old Market Place

The print below shows the Old Market Place about 1858 from Church Street with Messrs. Whitwhams on the extreme left with the gable end of the house of Mr. T. B. Parkes dominated by the tree in the garden (later the site of David Morrison & Son Estate Agents and now the Elite Dress Agency). Post Office Street as such, did not then exist at that point.

The Unicorn Hotel is clearly visible adjoining the old Town Hall built in 1849, (now part of the Unicorn). Note the oriel window of the Council Chamber, surmounted by the Town clock above which is the bell tower.

When the Buttermarket, erected in 1684 by Henry Lord Delamer, in the square was demolished, the old bell was transferred to the Bell Tower, above the old Town Hall. It weighed about 135 lbs. and now occupies a place of distinction for all to see inside the hotel near the foot of the staircase.

On the extreme right is No. 1 Church Street, the shop of H. Grange, chemist, whose verbose advertisement is shown on page 9.

Old Market Place (above)

This view was taken in 1906 and shows the site after it was redeveloped by Wm. Cunliffe Brooks, whose monument in the form of a copper heart-shaped weather vane with the initials W.C.B. cut out of the metal, originally appeared on the roof of this property and also appears today on the roof of David Morrison & Son's Auction Galleries and the Elite Dress Agency.

The flags on the building celebrated the occasion of the return of Lord and Lady Stamford to Dunham Hall in 1906.

The Poplars

Mrs. Boote's Cottage, Ashley Road, Altrincham (below)

This old thatched cottage must have been built in the 16th century of timber framing and thatched roof typical of so many in the area at that time. It was situated between Tadman's Cottage to which it was joined and the first of the new converted shops opposite the new office block. This cottage was for many years occupied by Mrs. Boote.

Tadman's Cottages, Ashley Road, Altrincham

Approached via steps through the bricked up door in the gable end of what was known as Tadman's Cottages was the first Sunday School in Cheshire started in 1783 by Oswald Leicester, the son of an Altrincham grocer. Ashley Road was then known as Thorley Moor Lane (house opposite still today called Thorley Moor). The site of this Sunday School is now occupied by an office block Byroe House. Oswald Leicester's father later built his son a School House and Lecture Hall in Normans Place, Altrincham about 1785. This School prospered and it was the first house on the righthand side of Normans Place and known as "The Poplars".

It was latterly used as a Private House by the Misses Griffiths until about 1973–74 when it was purchased by The Anchor Housing Association who demolished the house and erected a small development of elderly peoples flats of mature appearance and in keeping with the conservation area in which they stand.

The flats were opened by the Mayor, Councillor Fink in 1978.

They are still known as 'The Poplars', one flat of which is currently occupied by Miss Griffiths, the last surviving owner of the old house.

Oswald Leicester became the first incumbent of St. George's Church when it was erected in 1799 up to his death in 1832.

Byroms, Kingsway, Altrincham

Byroms, one of the oldest family concerns in the town, was established by Mr. James Byrom, who was Mayor of Altrincham in 1880, in a shop which once stood on part of the site now occupied by Lloyds Bank in Old Market Place.

In 1869 his son, J. W. Byrom, was apprenticed to the firm which by this time had removed across the road and lower down Kingsway and in 1886 on the death of his father, succeeded to the business. J. W. Byrom was much respected and liked and was Mayor in 1901 and welcomed the Lord Mayor and Sheriffs of London on their visit to inaugurate the extension to the works of Lynotype and Machinery.

On his death he was succeeded by his son, Mr. Jack Bryom, who loaned the basement of his store for use by the Altrincham Garrick Society. In the 1930's Jack Byrom was joined in business by his two sons Bryan and Basil. The firm closed down probably some 15 years ago. It was the first shop in the town to be fitted with electric light.

The front of the store was rich in Victorian beauty, the windows throughout possessing quaint twisted mullions terminating at the apex in a shaped capital. It was perhaps a little unfortunate that it adjoined the shop premises of The Flamborough Head and Filey Bay Fish Company!

Lower George Street, Altrincham,

An interesting view of Lower George Street 1910, originally known as Well Street, showing some 16th Century Thatched Cottages opposite the old Library.

The tall building on the right comprised some small shops and the Police Lock-ups, above the entrance to which were two stone lintels engraved "Altrincham Police Lock-ups 1838".

In the distance can be seen Springfield House (now demolished) near to which was the large well from which the residents of Victoria Street, originally named Well Lane, and around drew their water. It was known as Big Well and was a noted centre for local gossip.

In one of these cottages lived Mr. William Ashley, overseer of the Parish. It was hereabouts that Carely Royle lived. He was a horse breaker and an interesting character who sharpened his appetite each morning by consuming two quarts of porridge for breakfast.

The street immediately behind The Malt Shovels Hotel was known as Police Street, as it lead to the Police lock-ups adjacent to the old Public Hall in 1838. The lintels have been kept for integration into the redevelopment of the Northern end of town. Police Street was commonly called Back o'th Barn, as there used to be an old barn at the rear of the Malt Shovels.

Left: Lower George Street

Original Faulkners Arms about 1858–75

The building on the extreme left was the Old Orange Tree Hotel, number 3 Railway Street, owned about this time by Martha Howard, which was demolished about 1880, when Stamford New Road was formed. The name was then apparently transferred to The Orange Tree Hotel, Old Market Place. In its place rose the Stamford Hotel and the premises of Thomas Faulkner, Beerseller, 5 Railway Street, were demolished on the construction of the New Road. Note the angle at which it adjoined the Hotel, hence its removal to enable a straight road to be formed.

Faulkners premises stood at a point in the road where some small coal offices and Mr. Sowerbutts, the florist's shop, stood near the corner of Grafton Street, now the entrance to The Mall.

To commemorate this historic and quaint old building the pub across the road near to Stella Brooks Fashion Shoe Shop was built and named "The Faulkners Arms".

Below:

Lady Jane Grey and her brother Roger on the lawn in front of Dunham Hall. The two ladies and the gentleman behind Lady Jane are Mrs. Lewis, Miss Aucland and Mr. Curtis Sparkes, whose family continues to live in the district.

The Stamford Family

The Earl and Countess of Stamford, returning along Market Street, Altrincham, with their son Roger and his sister Lady Jane Grey (now Lady Jane Turnbull) on their return to take up residence at Dunham Hall in June 1906. The offices of the old Board of Health can be seen in the background.

William Grey was born on 18th April 1850 in Newfoundland and took the title 9th Earl of Stamford in 1890. Five years later he married Elizabeth Louisa Penelope daughter of Rev. Charles Theobald, Rector of Lasham, Hants.

Upon his Father's death, Roger Grey became the 10th and last Earl and Lord of the Manors of Altrincham, Dunham Bowdon, Carrington and Bollington, in a long lineage, stretching back to before 1460. He never married and the title became extinct when he died on the 18th August 1976 at the age of 79, his funeral being held at St. Marks Church, Dunham Massey on 26th August 1976. His sister, Lady Jane Turnbull, who lives in London, takes a lively interest in all that is currently happening at Dunham. It is interesting to note that she was until her marriage in 1927 to the Rev. Peveril Hayes Turnbull, the last Lady Jane Grey. The First Lady Jane Grey was the eldest daughter of the 3rd Marquis

of Dorset. She was Henry VII's great granddaughter. The Hall and Estate not otherwise disposed of passed to the National Trust, who are restoring the Hall to its original glory and it should be open in early 1981 to the general public.

Little do the present generation realise how much they owe to Lord Stamford. He possessed an intense civic pride and an unmatched knowledge of this county. He loved the open Parkland and the majesty of the trees which give the centre walk through the Park a cathedral atmosphere. His concern for the future well being of the area was most noticeable in the way he

prevented anyone out to desecrate the district for his own ends.

Canon Ridgeway in closing his address at Lord Stamford's funeral correctly summed up the late Earl, when he said:–

"Lord Stamford has died. Altrincham and beyond will be the poorer for his passing. They will also be much richer for his living. May his Soul in Christ find peace and bliss."

Above:

The Countess, Lady Jane Grey, her brother Roger, whose hand clasps his Father, the Earl of Stamford, on the lawns in front of the Hall, at the reception to mark their return to Dunham.

Left:

A few well-known dignatories at the reception were; Mrs. Timperley of Dunham (seated) standing left Mr. A. Marshal Higham, Mr. Tom Johnson, Head Master of Seamons Moss School and on the right, Mr. Harry Yarwood, Mrs. A. Higham and Miss Elizabeth Higham.

Roger Grey 10th Earl of Stamford, his younger sister Lady Jane Grey and their mother Penelope, Countess of Stamford, outside Dunham Hall during the Great War.

Ashley Road (left)

Ashley Road, Altrincham was once known as Thorley Moor Lane to which stands testament a stone gate post opposite Byroe House bearing the name Thorley Moor.

This view was probably taken about 1912 after the road had been widened from a rough track through the generosity of Mr. J. H. Broun who purchased the whole of the land including that lying West of Willowtree Road up to Ashley Road and made a gift of a strip of land to enable Ashley Road to be widened at this point.

Mr. Broun built all the terraced houses on the lower side of Willowtree Road and was also responsible for the erection of Station Buildings, Altrincham.

On the corner of Ashley Road and Hale Road is situated The Wilson Rest Garden given to the town in 1933 by Albert and Hilton Wilson in memory of their Father John Beech Wilson, who established The Bon Marche in Railway Street.

Oldfield Hall and John Leigh Park

In the 14 acres of John Leigh Park, Oldfield Lane as we now know it, once stood a red sandstone classical style mansion known as Oldfield Hall, probably built by the 2nd Earl of Warrington about 1666. Sir George Booth died there in 1684, also his second wife in 1690.

Many well known people have lived there including Jeremiah Lloyd (see Altrincham Hospital) and later in 1892 James Grimble Groves M.P. for Salford and who was Mayor of Altrincham in 1897 and 1898. After he left, it remained empty until 1916 and a year later it was purchased by Sir John Leigh M.P. who then gave it to Altrincham District Council as a permanent open Park.

Many local Coal Merchants possessed their own Railway trucks, which carried the coal from pit-head to the Local Depot at Altrincham. One such was James Horley, whose old established business was continued after his death by his son Edward J. Horley.

The young man at the back was responsible for putting the loose load of coal or coke from the cart into the customer's coal place. There were no sacks. Each load averaged 1½ tons for which he was paid 1s. 3d. or 1s. 6d. (about 7½p). Sometimes it had to be wheeled in a barrow a distance of 50 yards or more. At some of the larger Bowdon houses, he was offered a gratuity of 6d (2½p) and a piece of bread and cheese and tea, or beer.

Edward Horley was the first of a long line of Presidents of The District Traders Association to wear a Presidents Medallion in 1931 when the association was renamed The Altrincham Chamber of Trade.

Edward, apart from being a well-known local photographer, became an Altrincham Alderman. He was Mayor of Altrincham in 1956 to 1957. He died 24 June 1975 having been born at 44 The Downs, where he lived for 8 years before moving to No. 35 The Downs up to the time of his death.

The Bricklayers Arms (right)

The Bricklayers Arms, Beggars Square, George Street, Altrincham in 1870, perhaps still one of Altrincham's quaintest and most popular pubs, managed at that time by James Drinkwater, the Pub is little changed but more handsome to-day.

It was flanked by the cottage of Mr. Bagnall (a clogger) and on the left by the Altrincham and Broadheath Corn Mill offices which were demolished in 1908 to become the site of the Salvation Army H.Q. in Altrincham. The building they erected at the rear of the site was later demolished and the present H.Q. backs on to Central Way. The long front garden to the old H.Q. was then sold for the erection of a modern store fronting George Street and adjoins the Bricklayers Arms.

St. George's Church Altrincham

Built in 1799 but enlarged in 1858, its first incumbent was Rev. Oswald Leicester, whose philanthropic work throughout the area was well known. In 1886 a chancel was added. Considerable rebuilding operations took place and were completed about 1897. It became the Parish Church of the Altrincham Court Leet, Mr. Wm. Griffin, who was Mayor in 1893–4 being the first Mayor to set the example of attending morning service on the first Sunday after the Mayor making, a custom which continued until amalgamation into Trafford. in 1974. He also arranged the First Mayors Ball for children and gave a new livery to the Town Crier.

Above:

This group taken in January 1911 could have been a football team connected with St. Margarets Church, Altrincham, for the then vicar The Rev. Hewlett Johnson (later known as The Red Dean), featured 3rd from left back row with George Jackson well known fishmonger on The Downs. On his left also Marshall Higham first left middle row. Others depicted include A. Sheppard, L. Bowland, Bob Gregory, A. Lofthouse and Percy Dean.

Hale Moss

The whole of the area known originally as Hale Moss stretched from near The Moss Hotel in Moss Lane westwards as far as Railway Street and comprised some 60 acres in extent. The boundary between Hale and Altrincham bisected the area and right through the middle of the 19th century up to just before 1900, Gypsies camped there and could be seen making clothes pegs and weaving baskets; the area being looked upon as Common Ground for grazing, tipping etc. It was all re-claimed in 1906.

In 1880 Lord Stamford gave the present site of Stamford Park to the Town following which the Council landscaped the area of some 16 acres at a cost to the ratepayers of about £7,500. King George the V Pool behind the gas works is perhaps the last remaining evidence of what was once Hale Moss.

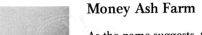

Money Ash Farm

As the name suggests, this old brick built thatched roof cottage originally stood near Money Ash Road and occupied a position roughly where York Street (off Lloyd Street) is situated.

At about the time of this photograph it was occupied by James Skelhorn, a coal and general dealer. Through the opening to the left can just be discerned the wooden railings bounding the railway bridge at this point.

23

The Stamford Estates Office

Perhaps one of Altrincham's fairest buildings, erected in 1780, possessing all the charm and dignity of the late Georgian Period, it is now a listed building.

It was at the time the home or office of one Isaac Worthington, a Solicitor and in 1835 the premises were occupied by Messrs. Nicholls Harrop & Worthington (now Messrs. Nicholls, Lindsell & Harris) who later moved to their present position in Market Street.

The offices were later occupied for many years by The Earls of Stamford up to the time of the last Earl's death in 1976 when the National Trust came into possession of the Estate.

On the right of this picture can be seen the shop of J. Richardson, Cycle & Motor Dealer with its corner date stone . . . UNITY Building 1897. He was later to move across to Dunham Road opposite the Police Station where he erected a large showroom and premises known as Unity Garage. It is now a modern filling station.

Left:

The Altrincham Prize Band heading a procession followed by the Local Branch of the Independent Order of Oddfellows entering Railway Street from George Street with the Woolpack Hotel on the left and The Stamford Hotel on the right. About the time of the outbreak of the First World War.

Above:

The later view, about 1927–30, in the same position shows the procession of children from St. Vincent's R.C. Church through the town.

Stamford Estates Office

Railway Street (right)

Some interesting facts about Railway Street emerge from this photograph, which appears to have been taken just after the turn of the Century.

John Hewson Needham had been in business as a butcher at 34 Railway Street for many years, next door to number 32, actually occupied in 1899 by Benjamin Battman as a florist, grandfather to Cyril and his son, Nurserymen in Timperley in spite of the Frys chocolate advert on the window.

Mr. Battman vacated his shop followed soon after by Mr. Needham, who moved higher up Railway Street into premises now occupied by the Burnley Building Society.

This site was then sold to the Lancashire and Yorkshire Bank who erected the present fine sandstone building between 1896 and 1900 and is now used as an Art and Picture Gallery.

Note the inconvenient position of the sun blind across the bedroom window, necessitated of course by the very low height of the shop.

On the left are the premises of J. H. Dean, seed and wine merchants, who took into partnership George Wainwright, previously employed by Walkden and Downes, grocers on The Downs when the name of the firm became Wainwright and Dean.

We know this photograph was taken prior to 1907 when the tramway was opened, as there are no lines in the road.

The shop on the right was occupied at this time by Frederick Johnson, Jeweller and Watchmaker, since which time it has continued as a jewellers (now Lepps).

Library Extension Opening

Saturday 19th May 1928 was the occasion of the opening of the new Library extension (to the right out of picture) designed by the late Mr. John Cocker, opened by the Earl of Crawford and Balcarres (centre) and supported by Lord Stamford (2nd right), the Mayor and Mayoress (Mr. and Mrs. William Kayley) Alderman Sydney Garner (3rd right), Alderman William Biddle (3rd left), Miss Florence Beckett (Librarian in centre, and others.

Miss Beckett retired after 40 years service as Librarian and "The Florence Beckett" Lecture Hall was officially opened on 15th February 1934 by Councillor Thomas Clayton, Chairman of Altrincham Council as a tribute to her public service.

Altrincham Picture Theatre

Altrincham Hippodrome

Altrincham Garrick Society

The Society was formed in November 1913 by Walter S. Nixon with A. P. Hill, Solicitor as Treasurer. Headquarters were kindly provided by Mr. J. W. Byrom in the spacious basement beneath his Kingsway drapery store. It was here they established the little Cellar-Theatre. Many well known productions took place mainly at the Public Hall including "Gallows Glorious" by local playwright Ronald Gow.

It was some 20 years later when, fired by encouragement from George Bernard Shaw that the Garrick Playhouse began to take shape and proved to be the first Little Theatre built for its purpose in Great Britain.

It was designed by T. Harold Hill, built by Charles Pennington of Hale, and opened by P. M. Oliver, liberal M.P. for Altrincham, on 1st October, 1932 at a cost of about £9,000. It possesses some 500 seats, a stage wider than that in Manchester Opera House, and a car park for about 300 cars.

For the Society's first production in the new playhouse "Immortal Lady", the centre page of the programme was printed on transparent paper to enable the audience to read the names of the cast and the scenes by holding them up to the light from the stage.

Altrincham Picture Theatres

The first theatre in Altrincham of any note was the Central Theatre in Shaws Road situated near the corner of Central Way. For many years this prospered, later to be converted into a small cinema which closed in the early 1930's.

Meanwhile, in 1913 The Altrincham Picture Theatre was built as a cinema on the site now occupied by the modern office block Station House. It filled a long felt need during the silent days through to the coming of the "talkies" and was a popular Theatre, closing 1966 with the showing of the film "Von Ryans Express". Then followed the Hippodrome, Hale Cinema built in 1919 which was demolished in 1979. The Inland Revenue Offices at Roberts House, Manchester Road, Altrincham now occupy the site of the Regal Super Cinema, the last cinema to be built in the 1930's.

Above:

Altrincham Hippodrome in 1963 as it finally closed showing Sophia Loren in "Madam". Managed at that time by Frank Hargreaves whose Father opened the building originally as a live variety theatre described as Altrincham's Premier House of Entertainment, and where a box could be booked for 2 shillings per person, dress circle and stalls 1 shilling, pit 6d. and gallery 3d. Arthur Leslie (Jack Walker of Coronation Street) used to play here with Freddie Fox (later Altrincham's King Carnival). It re-opened after alterations as a Cinema (Studio One) and a Bingo Hall combined.

Altrincham Carnival 1927

This picture depicts the installation of the Rose Queen on the Devisdale, Bowdon, by the Mayor and Mayoress of Altrincham, Mr. & Mrs. D. Stanley Morrison, watched in the foreground by King Carnival (Freddie Fox) whose opposite number Queen Carnival (Ted Fleming) can be seen on the right of the picture.

The Carnival continued for a very long time and raised a great deal of money for Altrincham General Hospital and other charities until it terminated through lack of support.

In 1978 the Altrincham Festival Committee was formed and has grown in strength during the past two years to perpetuate the purpose of the old Altrincham Carnival, opened with a procession of colourful floats, bands, Morris dancers and continued throughout the week with a host of interesting events, raising large sums of money for local charities.

Below: The Mayor of Altrincham (D. Stanley Morrison) attending the departure of the Rose Queen, following her installation on The Devisdale in 1927.

Collegiate Institution & Boarding Establishment for Young Ladies

SPRINGFIELD HOUSE, ALTRINCHAM.

ESTABLISHED BY THE LATE SAMUEL OLIVER, M.A.

Conducted by

Mrs & Miss Oliver, assisted by the first Masters

Springfield House (left)

Springfield House, Altrincham, shown here as it appeared in 1855, was a picturesque Georgian House and was a Boarding School for young ladies, established by Samuel Oliver and continued by his wife and daughter for many years.

It occupied a site now adjoining the old Altrincham Hippodrome (Studio 1) and Springfield Road was later named after this house. As the years passed, it was later used for commercial purposes by The Pleasal Manufacturing Company, by Mr. Charlton and his Brother and latterly by Cartwrights the furnishers. It fell into disrepair and while being a "listed" building, no one was prepared to spend money on it and it was finally and sadly demolished in about 1978.

A modern block of offices is now rising on the site.

Distinguished Guests at Altrincham Agricultural Show 1927

Left to Right:
Lord and Lady Mayoress of Manchester, Mr. Eustace Parker, Sir Edwin and Lady Stockton, Lord Stamford, Sir Cyril and Lady Atkinson, Mayor and Mayoress of Altrincham (Mr. & Mrs. D. S. Morrison), Lord and Lady Mayoress of Salford.

Stamford Arms and Bowling Green Hotel, Church Street, Altrincham

At approximately the present site of Hamilton House, the office block in Church Street adjoining the Cresta Court Hotel, once stood this fine old white painted building originally known as The Stamford Arms and Bowling Green Hotel, a celebrated posting house run by John Wall. At the passing of the stage coach era, this became the private house of George Faulkner Armitage Esq., J.P. who was Mayor of Altrincham throughout the whole of the First World War 1913–1918. It was re-named Stamford House.

Amongst other attributes he was a fine woodcarver. The carving to the staircase at Hilston House, Green Walk, now a Cheshire County Home for Gentlefolk, in addition to carving to the choir stalls in Cheshire Churches, stands testimony to his skills.

It is also interesting to note that he designed the War Memorial Cenotaph which stood for many years outside St. Margaret's Church on the main road, but was later moved to a more attractive position in the Rest Garden immediately opposite the Church.

It was erected in 1920 and opened later that year by Mrs. Bradbury, the Mother of Altrincham's V.C.

Stamford Arms & Bowling Green Hotel.
JOHN WALL.

Billiard Room.

APARTMENTS FOR PRIVATE FAMILIES.

Altrincham.

SADDLE & HARNESS HORSES ON THE SHORTEST NOTICE.

JOHN WALL,

In acknowledging the kind and increasing Patronage bestowed upon him since entering on the above Hotel, wishes to state that no attention on his part shall be wanting to make the accommodation equal to any Family and Commercial Hotel in the Kingdom, none but articles of the very First class in every department are kept about the Establishment.

There is an excellent Billiard Room on the Premises, also one of the Finest Bowling Greens in the County attached.

The House commands a splended View of the Derbyshire and Staffordshire Hills and surrounding Districts, is Fifteen Minutes' Walk from the beautiful and picturesque Park of Dunham, and only Half an Hours drive to the well known Villiage of Rostherne.

N. B.—Excellent STABLING WITH LOOSE BOXES, LOCKUP COACH-HOUSES &c., and every accomodation for Gentlemen Hunting with the Cheshire Hounds.

Vehicles of every description with First rate Horses and steady drivers always on hand.

Public or Private Dinners got up on the shortest notice.

Cunliffe Brookes first bank

On the opposite corner of Woodlands Road (previously Bank Street) once stood this end terraced house No. 40, Church Street. Before Bank Street was formed this area was an open field and this house was occupied by a Solicitor, Mr. William Pass, whose family was very well known then in Altrincham. Later, the house was occupied by Cunliffe Brookes & Company who were bankers and when the street at the side was formed, it was given the name Bank Street. This was later changed to Woodlands Road, presumably after Cunliffe Brooks had moved in 1877 to their new premises in Old Market Place, later to become Lloyds Bank. This photo was taken about 1935.

Jacob Bowland established his Decorating and Painting Business here at the corner of Normans Place and Regent Road in 1879, the entrance to the shop being in Normans Place. The earlier of these two photographs was probably taken just after the turn of the century, for it was in 1910 that Jacob built the extension forward into line with the adjacent cottages on the ground floor only in the case of the two lower shops and on ground and first floor in the case of his own shop. Unfortunately he died before it was completed. The business was continued however, by his son, and later his grandson, who retired about 1972 and now lives in Normans Place.

Note in the later photograph the Old Chapel has been demolished to make way for Regent Road Car Park. Doubtless John Wesley, who preached here in 1790 at the age of 87 years would turn in his grave if he could see the new Ladies and Gents Toilet built on the actual site of the Old Chapel.

Regent Road was known as Chapel Walk following the opening of the Methodist Chapel in 1788.

Goose Green

An old resident of Goose Green was Mr. Isaac Garner, a shoemaker, whose fine breeds of Geese garnished many a Christmas table . . . Hence the name, Goose Green.

Another resident of the Green was Mr. James Smith, famous for his crops of early potatoes which had a wide reputation in the Markets, as Bowdon Downs Potatoes.

In another cottage dwelt Mr. George Barlow, who made blacking and spent Saturdays delivering it to his customers, in order that their shoes might be bright for Sunday, when they went to hear the sermons of Parson Oswald Leicester the first vicar of St. George's, the Parish Church of Altrincham, built in 1799.

Altrincham Market

Probably one of the last remaining benefits granted to the town in the Charter of 1290 is Altrincham Market. An inheritance from the dim past, upon which the importance of Altrincham was built, and an institution which today is not only a valuable income asset, but is the envy of thousands who have visited here from home and abroad, who are amazed at the colour, the bustling busyness and the service given by those concerned.

Originally this was a Tuesday only market and a fair of three days, later changed by Edward II to the Feast of St. James, later known as Sanjam Fair, which lasted from 1319 until 1895 when it was abolished by the Home Secretary.

The Market Tolls and Powers, hitherto granted to Lord Stamford, were conveyed to The Local Board of Guardians, who in 1880 erected the present market hall, at a cost of just over £5,000. Over the years its popularity increased and in 1930 the whole of the adjacent land was enclosed with a glass roof on iron pillars. It was not until 1932 that the Council agreed to a Saturday market in addition to Tuesday.

Altrincham's Colourful Characters

Old William, Watercress Jack and Peter Weazle were noted characters who frequented the Pig Market adjoining the Old Axe and Cleaver Hotel, Beggars Square, George Street and Altrincham Market in the 1870's.

Fancy Dress Parade

The occasion of a Fancy Dress Parade towards the end of the Boer War from Old Market Place to The Devisdale and shows Jack Byrom (left) as Robinson Crusoe, William Heptonstall (centre), (brother-in-law to George Nixon of Burston and Nixon, Grocers, Hale) and Beatrice Hall (right), later to become the wife of Marshall Higham. The Troops were advancing on Pretoria which perhaps explains the banner across the handlebars of Miss Hall's cycle.

A welcome sight in the Town Centre in the 1920's was Mrs. Margiotta who regularly ground out her peculiar melodies in the Town Centre. Sometimes she had a monkey on a string and at other times a highly coloured bird in a cage.

Seen here in Stamford New Road, she lived round the corner in Chapel Street which was once between The Grapes Inn and the Wesleyan Chapel but now part of Regent Road car park.

Congregationalism struggled from 1803 to take root in Altrincham and not until 1839 did the movement take over this building at the foot of The Downs, a chapel built in 1830 and conduct regular services there. To this day can still be seen the Mezzanine floor, approached up a number of steps from the shops now existing beneath which was the place of Baptism and an examination of the frieze above the ceiling discloses the presence of Biblical Texts extending round the perimeter of what was the first Congregational Church.

As the congregation increased in size, larger premises were built and in 1848 services were transferred to the new church in Beechfield, Higher Downs, shown here.

This is a most attractive building in the Gothic Perpendicular design with much fine stone detail and beautiful stained glass windows. The pulpit was originally designed for St. George's Chapel, Windsor,

the Communion Table, part of which is made from wood from The Mount of Olives and the inlaid design of the cup and paten are from the Cedars of Lebanon.

The old building at the foot of the Downs was afterwards used as a day school and Sunday school. Later still the Presbyterians used it till their church was built in Delamer Road and finally it was used by the Baptists until their church was erected at the corner of Hale Road and Byrom Street.

While on the subject of Congregationalism, it may interest readers to learn that a much larger new school in Oxford Road, was built for £2,600 in 1873 called The British Schools. The Mackennal Institute adjoining was a later addition following the death of the Rev. Alexander Mackennal, who died in 1904 and who had done so much for Congregationalism, both here and abroad.

Poor and mean though it may have been, King George V is believed to have called it the Bravest little street in England because out of its 60 odd houses, no less than 161 men joined up, of whom 50 never returned in the First War.

The Roll of Honour can still be seen in the rest garden opposite St. Margarets Church and the panels which once surrounded it when it used to be fixed to the wall of the Chapel, are now on the first floor in Altrincham Town Hall.

The Site of Mothercare, George Street (right)

This was the site of 36 George Street, a private house approached by stone steps and iron handrail with corner shop adjoining, occupied by Collins and Warren apprentices to John Barrow malt, hops and ale dealers and grocers, in 1887. At about the turn of the century, Messrs. Coupe and Hilkirk purchased the site, demolished these buildings and erected a fine corner shop, succeeded by Stanley's Market. They sold the site to Mothercare, who erected the latest building on the site, one of the most valuable corners in the town.

Beating the Bounds 1901

(Left to right) J. BROOKS, A. GRIFFITHS, J. T. HUGHES (OVERSEERS) and G. E. TURTON (ASSISTANT OVERSEER), T. PRITCHARD (RELIEVING OFFICER), W. S. STOKOE (CLERK TO U.D.C.), CHAS. NICKSON, EDWARD BRADLEY, GEORGE WORTHINGTON.

Beating the Bounds started centuries ago and is really lost in the mists of antiquity. It was an ancient custom believed to have been carried out at Rogation Tide and was originally for the purpose of blessing the land and praying for a good harvest from the soil, particularly in the more agricultural areas, of which Altrincham was one.

This shows the overseers beating the Bounds in 1901 when it took two days to complete and necessitated in some cases, traversing through gardens of private houses.

St. Margaret's Church Vicarage actually lay in two Townships and on the boundary so that the overseers had to go through the vicar's study and drawing room in order to follow the boundary.

The vicar at that time was the popular and well liked Archdeacon Maxwell Woosnam, who provided the party with morning coffee. He was succeeded in 1908 by Rev. Hewlett Johnson (the Red Dean) who later became Dean of Canterbury.

The practice of beating the bounds then lapsed for 21 years. It was carried out again in 1922 since when it appears to have lapsed again until the Summer of 1980 when the re-constituted Court Leet revived this age old practice.

The significance of Road and Street Names in the area.

Over a period of many years it has been interesting to discover how many of the streets and roads about here come to be so named. Not all, but quite a number, stem from some connection with the Stamford family, as can be seen from these examples. Where known, details are also given as to how certain names were born.

DORSET ROAD

After the Marquis of Dorset, one of the Stamford family titles.

GROBY ROAD

Pronounced GROBY but correctly spelled GRUBY. The birthplace of Lady Jane Grey in Leicestershire.

BONVILLE ROAD

One of the Stamford family titles long ago extinct (see Harrington Road).

WOODVILLE ROAD

After Elizabeth Woodville who married Sir John Grey.

SUFFOLK ROAD

After the Duke of Suffolk, father of Lady Jane Grey.

BRADGATE ROAD

A village near Gruby, the home of Lady Jane Grey.

BENTINCK ROAD

After the 5th Earl's wedding to Lady Henrietta Cavendish Bentinck second daughter of William 2nd Duke of Portland.

CAVENDISH ROAD

After Lady Henrietta Cavendish Bentinck.

DELAMER ROAD

After George Booth, 1st Lord Delamer. In 1684 the Town Bell was given to Altrincham by 2nd Lord Delamer and installed in the Bell Tower above the clock in the old Town Hall, (now the Unicorn Hotel) where the Bell is on the staircase.

PORTLAND ROAD

After 3rd Duke of Portland a forebear of Lord Stamford.

BOOTH ROAD

GREY ROAD

After George Booth Earl of Warrington and Lord Grey.

ENVILLE ROAD

An estate in Staffordshire (now extinct) once owned by Lord Stamford.

HAMON ROAD

MASSEY ROAD

CHARTER ROAD

After Hamon De Massey to whom the Altrincham Charter was granted in 1290.

HARRINGTON ROAD

After the marriage of Elizabeth, daughter of Henry Grey Earl of Stamford and Baron Bonville and Harrington.

ELCHO ROAD

After the 6th Earl of Stamford's marriage to the daughter of Francis, Lord Elcho.

CATHERINE ROAD

Probably after the second marriage of the Earl of Stamford to Catherine, daughter of Henry Cocks.

LANGHAM ROAD

After Henry Lord Delamer who married Mary daughter of Sir James Langham.

WOODCOTE ROAD

After the 6th Earl's sister Maria who married John Cotes of Woodcote, Salop.

DE QUINCEY ROAD

After Thomas De Quincey (1785–1859) who described Altrincham so graphically in his notes.

REGENT ROAD

Originally known as Chapel Walk in 1760 extending from Railway Street up to Normans Place beyond which it was known as Garden Walk up to Groby Road. It was renamed Regent Road after the Prince Regent, who visited Altrincham between 1810–1820.

WAINWRIGHT ROAD

After Canon F. Wainwright M.A. the first Vicar of St. Johns, who completed 50 years service in 1915 and later at Bollington.

WILLIAM STREET

TIPPING STREET

POWNALL STREET

YARWOOD STREET

HEATH VIEW

ROSTHERNE STREET

Named after Elizabeth Pownalls Grandson, William Tipping Pownall, who lived at Yarwood Heath, Rostherne.

GARDEN LANE

(off Victoria Street) and still in existance. Named after the old Pear Tree Gardens adjacent to which stood the Old Pear Tree Tavern. Now a service road to the rear of the Church Street shops.

WELL STREET

Latterly known as Lower George Street and extended from the end of George Street to the junction with Stamford Street by the Malt Shovels Inn.

POLICE STREET

Extended along from a barn at the rear of the Malt Shovels Inn to the rear of the old Police Lock-ups in 1838 adjacent to the Public Hall. It was sometimes referred to as Back O'th Barn.

KINGSWAY

The upper part was originally known as Stamford Street up to 1908. It was changed by petition to Kingsway being the principal thoroughfare traversed by the King and Queen when Prince and Princess of Wales on their way from Tatton Hall as Lord Egertons guests, to Altrincham Station to open the Manchester Exhibition in 1887.

That section of Kingsway opposite the Axe and Cleaver was known as Post Office Place as the corner shop between Kingsway and Lower George Street was a Post Office. It was later occupied by Mark Bowen, Ironmonger. When Kingsway was so named, the side street leading round the side and rear of the National Westminster Bank and coming out into Market Street, was named Post Office Street as it is today.

HEALD ROAD, BOWDON

(joins Langham Road and Stamford Road, Bowdon.) According to Dodgson, spelled HIELD, or, HELDE meaning The Hill Slope.

LLOYD STREET ALTRINCHAM

After Jeremiah Lloyd who built Lloyds Fever Hospital in Newtown.

BEACONSFIELD ROAD

After The Right Hon. Benjamin Disraeli, Earl of Beaconsfield, whose nephew's son Mr. Conningsby Ralph Disraeli, became Member of Parliament for Altrincham in 1895.

SPRINGFIELD ROAD

After Springfield House, once occupied as a young ladies boarding school, a fabric warehouse and latterly a curtain manufacturer, now demolished with an office block rising on the site adjoining the Old Hippodrome Cinema – corner of Stamford Street.

MOSS LANE

Extended from near the centre of Hale Moss a low lying area, once marshland but since reclaimed, past the football ground, over the railway to Stamford New Road. It continued at one time across the road into what is now Cross Street, at one time known as Ham Lane.

WOOD STREET

Another short street off Stamford New Road between Millers of Chester (Taylor & Cross) and the National Westminster Bank.

GROSVENOR ROAD

(alongside the Railway near the crossings.) Originally named Stamford Road in 1852 until the opening of Stamford New Road when it was renamed.

POT STREET

The very short length of cobbled street still existing, connecting Market Street with Greenwood Street between the glazed market and the hospital out-patients department.

NAVIGATION ROAD

On the 1852 Town Map, it was known as Stamford Road and must have been a continuation of Grosvenor Road (also previously Stamford Road). Navigation Road runs parallel with the canal at this point.

The old Packet House Inn and the original Navigation Inn are also clearly shown.

CHARCOAL LANE

The area near the entrance to the first park known as Molly Charcoal's Pit where there was once a Highway Robbery and where few people dared to go after darkness.

ST. MARGARETS ROAD

Originally known as Turf Lane – until St. Margaret's church was built by the Earl of Stamford and Warrington and consecrated in 1855.

VICTORIA STREET ALTRINCHAM

Originally known as Well Lane due to its proximity to a well situated somewhere opposite the old library. (See Well Street.) It was renamed to commemorate the accession of Queen Victoria. The old Roebuck Inn stood then as now at the top of the street.

Siddeleys Brewery, Peel Causeway, Hale – 1907

John Siddeley lived at Spring Bank House, Stamford Street, Altrincham (now the site of Studio 1 Cinema – The Old Hippodrome). A well known colourful character, he was made Mayor of Altrincham in 1878 and owned this not very salubrious brewery, built in 1866, outside the entrance to the Hale Station, where he brewed his beer not surprisingly known amongst the locals as "Siddeleys Purge". He also owned a small Pub called "The Rising Sun" where his beer was sold behind The Malt Shovels in Police Street, then known as Back O'th Barn on the counter of which was kept within easy reach of his customers, the large key to the outside toilet!

Hale Urban District Council purchased the brewery in 1907 by Auction for £1003 and in 1908 the garden site was laid out dominated by the Victorian Gothic Fountain and Horse Trough built in Macclesfield Stone to the memory of a keen animal lover George Baker Walsh. With the passing of the Horse Drawn Cabs, the Horse Trough was removed.

The cottages between the Railway Inn and Spring Road were purchased by Mr. W. Berry who erected the existing row of good shops. He was a Blacking Manufacturer, who lived at "Parklands" Charcoal Road, Bowdon.

Below: Hale Station

BROADHEATH
Congregational Church.

Popular Saturday Concerts.

Sixth Concert of the Twelfth Season
WILL BE HELD ON

Saturday, November 7th, 1914

In the Schoolroom,
NAVIGATION ROAD.

Programme provided by Miss C. J. Edgell and Friends.

ARTISTES:
Soprano, Miss L. BOURNE.
Contralto, Miss F. WARRENER.
Baritone, Mr. S. W. EDGELL.
Elocutionist, Miss C. EDGELL.
Banjo, Mr. H. BOWMAN.
Comedy Duettists, Miss C. Edgell and
Mr. S. Cheetham.
Humorists, Mr. S. Morrison & Mr. J. Murray.
Accompanist, Mrs. R. LAMBERT.

Chair to be taken at 7-30 p.m., by Councillor J. TADMAN, J.P.

Doors open at 7 p.m.   Admission up to 7-20, Side Entrance, Twopence ;
after 7-20, One Penny.

PRINTERS LIMITED, ALTRINGHAM.

How to spend a penny in 1914

An interesting Show Bill at the time of the
First War. All the Artists taking part were
well known, particularly Miss Connie
Edgell, Mr. Stanley Edgell, Mr. S.
Cheetham (Coal Retailers).

Miss Lillie Bourne was for years Post
Mistress at Market Street, Alt. Post Office, a
member of the North Cheshire Operatic
Society, the Garrick, other organisations
also Mr. Stanley Morrison and others.

The Broadheath Blockade

Broadheath Bridge (left)

An unusual view of the bridge spanning the
Bridgewater Canal at Broadheath.
Originally commissioned by the Duke of
Bridgewater in 1765 and built like all
Brindley structures, narrow and hump-
backed. In 1830 it was widened on both
sides and in 1907 it was widened still
further. Then in 1935 it was re-opened
again for use having been completely
rebuilt for £17,017.15s.1d.

The Broadheath Blockade

We are inclined to think of picketing as a
modern phenomenon but these men appear
to be in deadly earnest at the time of the
Broadheath Blockade about 1905.

Note the tremendous weight of the stone
blocks on the 3 lorries the shafts of which
had been removed to immobilise the lorries.

PORTER.

LD COTTAGES, BOWDON

Church Brow Cottages, Bowdon

About 90 years ago the upper cottage of this quaint little corner of Bowdon was occupied by a Miss Lightfoot. She and her sister once owned a thatched cottage and garden higher up known as Lightfoots Tea Garden. The site was later developed and became Bowdon Police Station.

Much later on in the second cottage, originally one house, lived Mr. Sutton, well known caretaker at Bowdon Assembly Rooms and previously groom to Colonel Behrens.

Below him lived John Hassall (on right of picture) who 94 years ago was a porter and haulier at Alderley's Farm, Bowdon.

In the next cottage dwelt Miss Peckett, who permissively took in Will Cartwright, a hosteler at The Stamford Arms Hotel, to live with her.

John Nixon, coachman at Hill Carr, St. Margaret's Road, lived in the next cottage, whose daughter-in-law won many prizes for her floral decorations.

In the fifth cottage lived Ann and John Taylor, teamsman at Alderley's Farm.

The cottage below the passage was thatched up to 1914 where lived Mr. Broom, head gardener to Abraham Haworth, Hilston House, Green Walk, now a County Council Home for the Elderly.

Left: Church Brow Cottages

Moss Cottage, South Downs Road

Situated at the corner of Marlborough Road nearly opposite Bowdon Cricket Ground can be found this quaint old memorial to the past but beautifully preserved and modernised with the existing cottage, little changed and with its beautifully thatched roof.

According to the carved lintel above the dormer window at the front, it was built in 1666 by Robert Leslie and his wife and was originally known as Leslie's Cottage. This cottage must at one time have been connected with Moss Farm opposite.

Bowdon Water Tower

Looking across Bowdon Lawn Tennis Club courts at the rather unsightly octagonal Water Tower built about 1874 by the North Cheshire Water Comany. In the distance can be seen the rear of the houses on The Firs, Bowdon behind which was situated a partially underground reservoir on the Devisdale.

The tower was demolished due to modernisation of piped water supply in 1930, the reservoir continuing in use until about 1955 following which the site was filled in and conveyed back to Lord Stamford in 1970.

Timperley

The Old Hall Hotel on Stockport Road, originally an old Manor House known as Timperley Old Hall, later became a private golf course and subsequently opened as a Municipal club on 1st January 1935 by R. H. Lee, Chairman of the Urban District Council.

Christ Church, Thorley Lane, Timperley was opened in 1849, the first incumbent being the Rev. Edward Dowling while much later in 1931 the Church of St. Hugh of Lincoln at West Timperley was opened to relieve the pressure at St. Vincents, Altrincham, brought about by the rapid growth of Timperley at that time.

Many of the roads were named after famous families concerned with the Manor of Timperley – Riddings Road, Gerrard Avenue, Vaudrey Drive, to name only a few.

Forest School Timperley, a well known and very successful Private School was founded in 1924 by the Misses Clegg in a house across the road from which they moved to the present premises. It is interesting to note that the four "houses" of the school are named NIMWOOD, CHORLTON, KERSAL and JORDAN after the names of the first 4 pupils to enter the school.

Timperley originally sported 3 pubs in close proximity – The Railway Inn at Aimson Road, The Church Inn (now Charles Court) and The Naked Child later re-christened The Stonemasons Arms, the latter by reason no doubt due to the Stone Quarry (now Marstons, the Builders). Again immediately opposite is the Quarry Bank Inn.

Uriah Arnold used to have a Stonemasons business where Jacksons Garage is situated.

Every keen local Sportsman knows that Timperley Cricket Club, which is the 3rd Oldest in the N.W. started in 1877 and the Hockey Section, the oldest club in the N.W. followed later in 1886. The Tennis Section was born just before the Great War. The whole club can field 20 teams of Ladies and Gentlemen from all its sections. The Ground, like the Municipal Golf course adjoining is owned by Trafford Borough Council.

Another well known institution, Timperley Agricultural show commenced in 1943 and ran for years until 1952 in a highly successful way under the able chairmanship throughout of Frank Gibson OBE, a well known Altrincham ex-Mayor under whose auspices the show was able to present £700 to Altrincham General Hospital.

Turnpike Cottage on the corner of Wood Lane and Stockport Road.

Near the old entrance to Woodlands Park

Timperley Old Hall